THIS GOES WITH THAT

SELECTED POEMS
1970 — 1990

Also by Peter Goldsworthy

Poetry

READINGS FROM ECCLESIASTES

THIS GOES WITH THIS

Short Fiction

ARCHIPELAGOES

ZOOING

BLEAK ROOMS

Novels

MAESTRO

THIS GOES WITH THAT

Peter Goldsworthy

SELECTED POEMS
1970 — 1990

An imprint of HarperCollins*Publishers*

*Collins/Angus & Robertson Publishers'
creative writing programme is
assisted by the Australia Council,
the Australian government's arts advisory
and support organisation.*

AN ANGUS & ROBERTSON BOOK

*First published in Australia in 1991 by
Collins/Angus & Robertson Australia*

*Collins/Angus & Robertson Publishers Australia
A division of HarperCollinsPublishers (Australia) Pty Limited
Unit 4, Eden Park, 31 Waterloo Road, North Ryde
NSW 2113, Australia*

*William Collins Publishers Ltd
31 View Road, Glenfield, Auckland 10, New Zealand*

*Angus & Robertson (UK)
16 Golden Square, London W1R 4BN, United Kingdom*

Copyright © Peter Goldsworthy 1991

*National Library of Australia
Cataloguing-in-Publication data:*

*Goldsworthy, Peter, 1951- .
  This goes with that: poems 1970-1990.*

  ISBN 0 207 16903 9.

  I. Title.

A821.3

Cover painting: **Dry Salvages** *(1956) by John Olsen
oil on hardboard 119 × 90.9
Gift of E.M. Gardiner in memory of her daughter Marie Gardiner 1972
Courtesy of Art Gallery of New South Wales
Typeset in Palatino 10/12 pt by Midland Typesetters, Victoria
Printed in Australia by Griffin Press*

*6 5 4 3 2 1
96 95 94 93 92 91*

AUTHOR'S NOTE

To publish a Selected Poems at an age which—to me at least—still feels like the first blush of youth is fortunately not without precedent, and my excuse is better than most: my first two books are both out of print, and my current rate of production is such that a third collection, even a collection as slim as the first two, is many years away.

This go-slow is only partly due to the belief that Less is almost always More. For despite this belief I have been attempting to fatten up my poems lately. One recent poem displaces about the same amount of page, and takes about the same amount of time to write, as four or five earlier poems.

This book offers an early excuse to publish these fattened poems, and thereby prevent myself tampering with them any longer—achieving what John Updike calls the 'sweetness of riddance'.

The arrangement of this selection is not remotely chronological, so as to thwart any reader who may hope to find signs of improvement or deterioration with the passing of time.

ACKNOWLEDGEMENTS

Previously uncollected poems have been published in the National Library Pamphlet Poets Series, the *Adelaide Review*, the *Sydney Review*, various *Friendly Street Readers*, *Verse* (UK), *PN Review* (UK), *Quadrant*, and the anthology *The International Terminal* (University of Newcastle Press).

CONTENTS

Razor

Carving this same face
out of soap, each morning
slightly less perfectly.

Act Six

Act six begins
when the curtain falls,
the corpses arise,
the daggers are cleaned.

Act six
places Juliet in the supermarket,
Mr Macbeth on the 8.15.

In act six
Hamlet sucks a tranquilliser,
Romeo washes up

and death
is gentle and anonymous:
Lear's life-support
switched discreetly off.

The Blue Room

I sit on a warm stone step in a doorway
to the Blue Room, the Morning Room.

There is much bee-noise and the noise
of birds: the acoustics are fine in the Blue Room.

Usually it may have rained overnight
in the Blue Room: this clear aquarium air.

In the Blue Room there is always one dove
—*hidden here, hidden here*—

and many honeyeaters,
up for hours, loony as tunes.

Today the Blue Room is available.
I sit among ants, between bees,

amid designer vegetation:
fine-detailed, non-repeating,

in the Blue Room, the Morning Room,
the wide Waiting Room.

Psalm

Joy again after time
without, arriving today
from somewhere.

A great irrelevance of joy:
stupidly free of touch
and taste and rush.

Gland Trouble?
Hidden pharmaceutical
springs?

Or joy *pour la joie*,
boundlessly
groundless?

Whichever, no matter.
This I take as is, as
come: joy without footnotes,

first among things
I no longer wish fully
to understand.

Winter Piece

Our son splashes carefully home
from puddle to puddle,
deep stepping stones.

We walk a shout behind
watching from inside our clothes,
breathing small clouds into the sky.

Around us the hard economy of winter:
frugal colour schemes, and underfoot
the worn currency of leaves.

We wrap our clothes tighter,
sheltering our feelings:
this mundane candle-power of love,

these memories of warmth this morning,
our son between us in the bed,
the coins of rain spilling over the roof.

The Nice

The people I want near
when night falls
are the nice:

those who went
to Sunday School
and still say Grace,

those who wheel meals
from door to door,
unbiographied,

those who wept in *Lassie*,
and saw it again,
and wept again,

the middle-classed
and all their children,
sugar of the earth.

Of course there are risks
even here,
small but measurable:

lost Guides, bent Brownies,
sentimental blokes
who offer sweets from cars.

Or so I've read.
Even these I prefer
to find innocent

till proven innocent,
wanting only
to be home before dark

each night, among friends,
all those
on whom depends

the diminishing good of the world:
the shrinking membership
of the Club Nice,

the Club Decent,
even the Club
Goody Two-Shoes,

which I almost believe
would still have me
after all these years.

This Goes With That

Significance everywhere, you say, recalling
the day I smote my cheek against a wall
chasing a wide backhand, only hours
after threatening to punch you in the face.

Must all things be explained?
I mention the distribution of knife-wounds
seen once in a slab of flesh on a mortuary sink,
or the pattern of tea-leaves glued inside these cups.

I even show you this poem so far, these images
selected by hunch and coin-flip: Exhibits A, B, D . . .
Chaos gets on your nerves, you tell me. Besides,
it's obvious: this goes with that

and always will. Somewhere deep inside
the dangling seventh must resolve,
the laws of grammar will not be broke.
There are even numbers which predict

the swirling accidents of rising smoke,
or if there are not, scientific Americans
will soon discover them. We sit sipping tea
in silence. You scribble solutions in the margins

of *Mathematical Games*, I adjust my poem.
On a small screen in a corner a dog dies, our child
weeps. Not true, you tell her. Never happened.
But knowledge is no cure, or escape.

Sunset

Always this same finicky attention
to detail: the high smears of cloud,
obsessively ribbed and textured,
the studied back-lighting, the precise
colouring, as if by numbers,
panther-pink, pool-blue, shade-grey:

a gift, yes, but thoughtlessly exquisite, and
far too expensive ever to reciprocate.

Nocturne

Rain in the large
small hours, bulging
gutters and bladders.

We stand at an opened window:
woken, emptied, listening
to the textures of darkness,

the ear-braille,
the nose-braille,
the rain sprinkling down,

the perfumes of the earth
folded back on themselves,
and multiplied . . .

Remember that childhood trick?
The single leaf of paper
folded, and re-folded:

a sudden book,
very small, very thick,
unable to be torn.

We sniff the wet
of the garden.
Such strength in things!

The press of rain
on the earth, unseen.
The million-ply, tough layers.

A Small Bestiary

Gecko

Summer nights it trembles
at the edge of consciousness,

in the corners of flyscreens,
in the corners of my eyes.

Almost certainly it exists:
a tiny, nervous dinosaur,

a leather spider on a web
sticky with electric light,

clutching moths in its gums
just out of sight.

Skink

Leaf-rustle

in the corner
of an ear.

Movement
there, and

there:
fish-quick

through
the low world.

Brief
glimpses.

Unconfirmed
sightings:

sardine-skin,
Thalidomide-leg,

identikit parts
for a description

that is never
complete.

This, though,
once:

a single
shed tail-tip

left trembling
in the palm,

a proof,
or very nearly.

Bushflies

Somehow
they fall
through the sky

much
heavier than air
machines,

bumping
into scenery
like low-flying gravel.

Eat me
they glint
loudly:

glitter-blue,
panel-beater
green.

They overshoot.
They stall.
They lob

into mouths.
They wedge
down throats.

They cover
steaming mounds
like sequins:

unfit
to survive
by the billion.

Earthworms

When hands part the moist earth
they crawl away underfoot

Pale abandoned fingers
wrapping themselves

against steps that knock
or the soft concussion of rain.

Snug in their planet.
Swallowing it slowly through.

Bees

Bees
have small furry pelts
hard to keep from getting sticky.

Their languages
are dance and telepathy.

Inside each bee
is delicate machinery
a noisy watch mechanism.

Some kamikaze freely for the Empress.
Others, at the end, look back with pride
on an 8 oz jar in the supermarket.

Tiger Snake

You barely ripple
the earth's skin

glide with minimum involvement
through worlds of green.

A green hit-man
moving with detached murder

with the innocence
of all that kill.

You slide like a tongue
through a silence

heavy
with the instincts of fur.

A river of muscle
weightlessly flowing

hardly touching
a thing.

Ode to the Potato

O practical
potato,

vegetable
most like earth,

among elegant asparagus,
fashionable

you are unpretentiously
spud.

Tasting only of stone
you have nothing to hide,

are merely functional
a most puritanical root.

O wave your green flags
democratic potato,

you the equal
of any other
potato.

Tomatoes

Make no excuse
for the behaviour of tomatoes,
fruit grown soft and fat,
victims waiting for a mouth.

There is no sport in these:
plucking themselves
into the hand, eagerly
consenting to be food.

They give too willingly:
flop-bellies bursting
open, blooding the mouth
unspeakably.

They will never resist.
Kick salt in their eyes,
and pass me another.

Hands

Hand   is the correct word
for fisted and knuckly things
the body's noble proletariat
happy in their work   or not unhappy.

Hands   are the brain's right hands
ad lib spanner or vice   hammer or spoon
in gloves of sweat.

Hands   are finest engineering
tools of hinge and prong
metric fingered and wrinkle gripped.

Hand   is the correct word
for endless instinctive things
a catapult   a club
a kindergarten computer
a salty horoscope.

Hand   is the word
reaching across the limits of words
a frontier of touch   in the silence.

Five Sketches

1. Song Found in a Bottle

I drank with a sailor once.
Or with a few words of him,
as much as anyone.

He hid behind his eyes,
in a cabin of bone and muscle.
His life was long ago,

in Aberdeen, perhaps, or Bergen:
the booze had worn his memories
as shapeless as pebbles.

Marooned on our continent
he rode the bitumen swell
on trembling legs,

carrying the sea everywhere
in a brown paper bag.

2. Widow

I watch from the boundaries
of my yard. From territory
marked by mower and secateurs,
the occasional drunken piss.

My neighbour was eighty.
After loud parties,
or footballs in her roses,
our words would cross the fence.
One of us spoke a different language.

As they carry her out
her children arrive in taxi-trucks.
They pack her home into boxes.
They fold up her territory
and take it away.

3. *Brickie*

He slaps each brick
into the palm of the last:

stone fists,
loaves of earth.

His rhythms
are Music For Easy Listening

and two-minute poems
of race-callers.

Noon is a fierce kiln.
He shelters among pallets

with a bottle of lunch,
a pack of tailor-mades.

Some days walls are enough craft.
Some days he's almost one himself,

redder than his bricks,
hardening into afternoon.

4. *Ratepayer's Ode*

He walks through an afternoon
of sunlight and neighbours,
along avenues of home loans,
almost paid.

Slow flies bump at his face,
webs catch and itch.
The cosmetics of summer surround him:
the slow detonation of fruit trees,
the green shallows of lawn.

A paperboy rides towards him
throwing novels into every yard.
He unwraps the headlines and reads.
It is science fiction again.
It is always science fiction.

5. *Metal Worker*

He walks out of the pub at dusk,
boots around neck, bare toes
in a cool river of bitumen.

The world has shrunk within earshot:
its horizons vague as traffic
or the scattering voices
slowly losing definition.

He's replaced a dozen schooners of sweat.
Lucky even the foundry's memory
is soluble in beer, and tomorrow's
just the blurred recollection of yesterday:

spoondrains
in a road smooth with booze and dreams.

Autobiograffiti

1.

Between yes and no
there are some things,

my mother taught
in many ways.

Between the lines
(she sang) is space,

between the colours
black and white,

those other colours,
there.

Nothing
(she tucked and kissed)

is easily diminished,
three lines will never fit

in two, there is always more,
elsewhere.

The world (my darling
boy) has each name

outnumbered, each
Doing Word outdone.

It coarsens
the finest print.

It twists and hides,
(like you, Menace)
refusing to be dressed.

2.

Let's get physical.
I was born

in a small town
with a large graveyard.

There were four pubs
but five churches.

There was a six-pack
of grain-silos.

Each morning milk poured into billies,
unscalded. Each month

parcels arrived from the Country
Lending Library in the city.

There was a wall of china
on the dresser, and coins

of water spitting
on the surface of the stove.

Outside, the fields were always green
and gold, the sky was endless blue:

to use any other description
would be perverse.

3.

At school
I believed everything
I was told:

words, usually,
sentenced
heel and toe.

How high
they always sounded
from below.

And such a grip!
Like fairy-shoes,
autonomously

goose-stepping: left-
right, about-
face.

They fitted. They pulled
in directions.
They exhausted.

Still
they will not
be unlaced.

4.

What Did You Get For Mental?
my father sternly asked each night.
Ten, I said, and seldom lied.

I sat in his study after dinner
reading hidden comics and waiting
for the call: Show Me Your Homework.

In the drawers of his desk
where I was not permitted
I often found strange toys:

Latin grammars; cheque-book stubs
neatly tied; a blue inkpad and stamps
marking NOT NEGOTIABLE;

and once, in its own deep drawer,
a pencil, deep bruise-purple,
mysteriously marked: INDELIBLE.

To ask was to confess
but inside his Shorter Oxford, this:
incapable of being erased.

Someone Has Been Using My Stamp,
he announced that night. Someone
Has Broken My Pencil.

In my homework book
were purple bruises,
incapable of being erased,

and vast cubist cities,
legoed from just two words:
NOT NEGOTIABLE.

Confiscated, those blue-prints lie
in his desk-drawer still, perhaps,
sealed in a bag marked Exhibit A,

or B, or Z, and labelled, in Latin,
in his hand which never fades: whatever
you have written, you have written.

5.

Something less definite
than ambition

washed me down hard rivers
to the bitumen estuary.

Here was loud music
and the Sexual Evolution.

Here were smart cosmetics:
knowledge, thickly applied,

and sophistication,
a ratchet winding

one direction only,
ever more tightly.

I learnt to stack big words
in walls, heavy sandbags.

I forgot
how to say please.

Those were the days,
I knew then I would say later.

6.

And always this beating of the mask
more thinly: each worry-line
and glistening tear-track.

I am seeking only a quest, you say?
Don't interrupt, or raise your eyebrows
like inverted commas.

As for the claim that Perfection
recedes infinitisemally
with each incremental step closer:

enough. I have never believed in algebra,
its untouchable verbs. I have seen tricks
on blackboards, yet gone home knowing

that even parallel lines touch
eventually, for theirs is the kingdom
of the real, free from definition,

and one day this mask
will be indistinguishable
from the face beneath,

or no longer a mask
but the face itself, for which
there can be no further use,

and I will find myself
suddenly nearing shore,
among birds.

Moonta

My family shovelled the best oxide
from the earth a century ago;
from land greener than Cornwall,
a stony green desert of copper.

Now the graveyard presses them to ore:
rows of relatives never known,
their shared name catching at the throat
repeatedly, like the end-rhyme in a ballad.

A museum preserves likenesses.
Daguerreotypes of my father's grandfather,
blacksmith turned mayor.
Great-uncles scrubbed for sermons,

aunts bent great by toil;
all their possessions catalogued,
even their bed-pans become antiques,
the meagre heritage of democracy.

They left high pyramids of slag,
the rubble of a past long smelted;
a history still extractable, but uneconomic:
all of us being relatives, in the end.

Encounter Bay, Winter

1.

The coast
is a rind of shacks:
a narrow city in summer,
a ghost port in winter
the sea washes
and forgets.

2.

I have the weekend
to myself: short days
filled with weather,
with difficult fishing,
and jogging the crunchy
edge. Days spent lost
in the push and pull
of muscle, forgetting
how to think, even
forgetting speech,
the empty shacks of words.

3.

Nights mean slow food,
the warm gravity of bed.
And noises: the waves
trampling ashore outside,
a whiteness in the ear,

the land returning to coldness,
the muscles of the sea
forgetting and remembering.

4.

Morning:
cooking water
for the first pot.
Wind sucking at the door,
ripping windows,
stoning rain onto the roof.
Morning:
the flap of the mind
steamed open,
first cup for the day.

5.

Too soon
I am driving back to Mondays,
to the exhaustion of speech.
Why is it
whenever I notice
I am driving back
or arrived?

Leaving at the edge
the empty rooms of molluscs,
crab shells, broken armour:
deserted shacks
the sea washes
and forgets.

Yorke Peninsula, Easter

1.

I drive out ten years
from the city's heavy gravity,
from the safety of numbers;

returning to childhood,
to fields of sweat and dust,
scraps of eucalypt,
wheezing crows;

to the backyard of summer,
the brown brown grass of home.

2.

I mean nothing profound by this:
no sermon against the sheep-race of cities,
no speech in praise of grass.
I prefer asphalt.

I mean just going home on a long weekend,
driving back through monotonous fields,
or driving in circles
through the same fields again.

3.

I sleep in the car
in the sentimental night,
behind windscreens foggy with dreams.

Tired eyes alter the darkness
to the different geography of childhood:

warrens trapped, bushes climbed,
beatings given and received.

From each dead field
these harvests of memory.

4.

In the morning
sunlight reconstructs the world.

The sky is cold,
the kitchen windows shiver
in their fields.

In one of them I am a child,
the woodstove is alight,

and from the chimney
dreams drift and vanish like smoke.

Credo

I believe in the infinite line,
the straight line between points
and the equality of all right angles.
Amen.

I believe also
in narrowness and excellence.
In the importance of measurements.

I like to keep things
inside things. I like to keep
adequate records.
I like to gazette.

Of course I prefer nouns to verbs
the label affixed, unmoved.
I like to draw chalk-lines.

I believe in making lists.
In quartz clocks,
calendars, reminder calls, alarms.
I like the hours 9am and 5pm,
and taking to the weekend shapelessness with these:
hedge-clippers, edge-trimmers,
a lawn-mower on the lowest notch,
secateurs.

I like collecting things
and looking up their names in books.
I like Killing Jars.

Always I will prefer the unblemished butterfly
pinned to a mounting-board
in the hard cone of a 60-watt desk-lamp

to the tattered joy
circling in a column of a dusty sunlight
somewhere.

To the Mother Tongue

English, you seedy
House of Reps:

your absurd electorates
named Tyger and Greek Urn,

your constituencies
of Lovely Scenery!

Don't try to convince me
with nuances:

all those wheel-barrows,
rain-varnished,

those pairs of cycle-clips,
fine-detailed, inset.

As for Love—
what word is that?

Keep your feelings
to yourself, English,

squashed in your books
like centrefolds.

I refuse to believe
that the word is quicker than the eye,

or that these line-drawings,
these tiny, funny stick-shapes

might come flickeringly alive
read fast enough,

as if words were really thoughts,
as if *this* were the way we think:

the cartoon, fully animated,
of the book, of the life.

After Babel

I read once of a valley
where men and women spoke
a different tongue.

I know that any uncooked theory
can find its tribe,
but this might just be true:

for us there are three languages,
yours, mine, and the English between,
a wall of noises.

At times our children interpret,
or music connects our moods.
There are also monosyllables,

the deeper grammar of fucking,
a language too subjective
for nouns.

But even after conjugation
the tense remains the same:
present imperfect.

We take our mouths from each other,
we carry away our tongues,
and the separate dictionaries in our heads.

This, Though

Yes, I remember special things
reluctantly. I admit
to a stash of clippings,
a mantlepiece of shined trophies.
But it's the trivial I prefer:
remembrance of things past
bothering about.

Once I was good at this:
trained study habits.
My mind was fast and empty,
and knew the tricks:
acronyms, repetitions,
the crumb of madeleine,
the knot on the finger.
I planned to know everything.

The present seemed too
singular, too here-and-now:
a tiny township blinked
and missed. I always wanted
to be there and then.

I took notes, kept snaps,
swotted the textbook
of each passing moment
till it was tested, re-tested, rote.

But the mind has a mind of its own:
a vain pecking order of forgetting.
What remains is always chosen elsewhere:
selected joys, collected humiliations.

This, though: small comfort.
If I cannot remember everything
I can hope, one day,
for the perfect justice of nothing:
a complete, a fair and equitable
forgetfulness.

Arson

I burn your letters
at the edge of night
—an autumn bonfire.

Into the flames
go leaves fallen from trees,
and those brought in the post.

Garden prunings,
and the foliage of desks
—drafts of unfinished pain.

Slowly the flames contract
to a fistful of ashes,
a finger of smoke in the night.

Even the stars we see
are only a kind of memory,
already dead for years.

Alcohol

You are the eighth
and shallowest
of the seven seas,

a shrivelled fragmented ocean
dispersed into bottles, kegs, casks,
warm puddles in lanes behind pubs:
a chain of ponds.

Also a kind of spa,
a very hot spring:
medicinal waters to be taken
before meals, with meals, after meals,
without meals;

chief cure
for gout, dropsy, phlegm,
bad humours, apoplexy, rheumatism
and chief cause of all the same.

At best you make lovely mischief:
wetter of cunts,
drooper of cocks.

At worst you never know when to stop:
wife-beater, mugger of innocents,
chief mitigating circumstance
for half the evil in the world.

All of which I know too well
but choose to ignore,
remembering each night only this advice:
never eat on an empty stomach;

for always you make me a child again—
sentimental, boring
and for one happy hour very happy—
sniffing out my true character like a dog:
my Sea of Tranquillity,
always exactly shallow enough to drown in.

Jokes

Don't tell me jokes,
I know about jokes.
They think they are funny.
They think they can get away with things.

I don't know everything about them,
just enough. I know this:
that they refuse to be remembered,
slipping the mind's fingers,
a shoal of laughter, vanishing.

And this: that they hide still inside,
deeply. Delinquent poems,
absconders from custody.

Of course they think it a great lark,
sneaking back again and again:
the grenade of laughter,
then silence.
I prefer to find it tiresome.
And a little sad.
All that repetition!

Don't pigeon-hole me:
I appreciate a good joke.
I said appreciate, not laugh at.
For I will no longer laugh.
I will not answer their ridiculous summons,
I refuse to accept their subpoena.
Never again will I eagerly rip open
the scented envelope
filled with strange plastic.

There are only four jokes anyway:
the custard pie, and the breaking of taboo,
the game of words, and the thing
we are each most afraid of.

Give Me Some Kind Of Sign

You who have Crossed Over,
Gone Before, Passed On:
let's hear it from you, if.

Send news, please, of your Zone:
a dragged chain, a rapped table,
make free with Special Effects.

But no nuances: I am done
with coincidence, with statistics
that tease the limit.

I want the unambiguous reassurance
of terror. I want to wake
at night screaming, tonight.

Haunt me, spooks, flicker
my reading-lamp, repossess
my house, give me some kind

of hard evidence.
I feel so chill and lonely
without you.

The Operation

Becoming the person you have always been
inside cannot be rushed. For some the dressing up
in secret clothes at home—batiks and silks,
caftans, sarongs—is all they ever need.
For others, food comes next: vaguely Asian takeaway
in confidential brown paper bags. Only the brave
come out in public: sitting in shopfront restaurants
proudly becoming what they eat, stir-fry and rice,
and more rice, in small civilised portions. Wherever,
you must use only chopsticks, or the washed right hand
alone, and rise always from the floor still hungry,
feeling smaller already, and daintier, and more refined.
Soon the hormone shots will darken the skin.
Submit to these procedures first: the chest-waxing,
the lid-narrowing. And the nose-job, of course:
you are leaving Big-Nose Europe behind.
There can be no turning back; you are ready now
for The Operation. A foot of flesh, at least, must go: the whole
high pulpit of European condescension. Of course not everything
is height: you must learn again to look up, not down.
Courses should be taken in History and Language, in Chief
     Exports
and Rainfall and especially Climate: stirred by the wings
of strange, bright butterflies the monsoons are moving closer;
already the summers feel wetter, the winters hotter.
There is pain, of course, but there is also peace: a happiness
oddly free of itself, free of shag-haired Europe
and its doggy emotions. Dogs are for eating now,
with the careful, inscrutable manners of a cat.
Suddenly the bandages are off, and everything can be seen.
The world has gone as quiet as a Public Library.
Meditate for a time in the open sun, safe from zinc
and freckles, the last ice melting from your heart,
the brooding indoor races of the north at last forgotten.

Other Shames

Often I lie awake,
red-faced in the dark,
remembering words
mispronounced years before
in public: names of the great
mostly, and place-names,
and the usual French.
Trying to remember large
guilts is more difficult. Small
shames keep intervening,
little things that hide the big:
the silly boasts, found out;
the fibs, confounded, the jokes
begun and lost
halfway, like music
insufficiently rehearsed,
and all the desperate gossip
I have passed on, magnified,
before hardening stares.

Have I forgiven myself
the deep that lies beneath
this membrane of shames?
If so, don't say
you've forgotten:
I am relying on you
to remember,
and never forgive.

Choice

an imitation of Tadeusz Rozewicz

Neatly place a V
by those qualities
you consider
to be vices

whereas

by those qualities
you consider
to be virtues
neatly place a V.

Games

after Vasko Popa

1. *Draughts*

This is not chess.

No trench of pawns.
No skulking
hierarchy.

Here only a flat world
of flat equals.

A dream
that hard work
makes any counter
King.

A road
from black to white.
From day into night.

2. *Musical Chairs*

When the music stops
grab two chairs,
one for your feet.

Shoot anything that argues.

Never forget the Rule:
No Spitting on the Battlefield.

The game is over
when there aren't enough players
to go around.

3. *Snakes and Ladders*

There is a snake
after every ladder.

A valley after every peak.
A morning after
after every night.

This can be read
in any Sanskrit text,
in any comic book,
in the bitter, salty lines
on any palm.

There is a snake
after every ladder.

Just believe
there is another ladder
after that.

Three Parodies

1. Quintets for Twiggy

after Les Murray

Is it possible
that puffing up Parnassus
you have neglected to pay tribute
to the Boutique Age aristocracy?
I refer to the skinny.

We were probably the last
civilised humans. Tribesfolk exposed us
on hillsides for good reasons.
We were sickly.
Out of self-defence

we invented the chic of tuberculosis,
gaunt salon elegance (See Gautier,
via Sontag: 'I could never accept
as a lyric poet
anyone weighing more than 99 lbs.')

We were the last of the oppressed
to come out: latent consumptives, phthisics, weaklings.
Not that the lists of pugnacity
are bare of thin fellows. Ask Bruce Lee.
Goliaths taunt us still,

kick sand in our eyes, fear us.
In war we're apt to be the snipers.
Our preferred weapon: the sling
of the tongue,
sharpened words at three paces.

2. Travelling to Alsace-Lorraine

after Andrew Taylor

For Beate

Darling, it seems that all our journeys end in the idea
of a forest, somehow. Rain falls in that forest,
and if we turn up our face we find,
once again, that it is wet rain.
Remember the wetness of the rain in Buda,
on the Danube, and how similiar it was in Pest?
Last year I travelled to Zagreb, solo,
and it was also raining, and the rain was wet.
Here among the damp pines have sprung mushrooms
that only you can identify.
They cluster in bright teams, like Rapid Vienna,
or Moenchengladbach.
You pick handfuls, glazed with rain,
for a quiche. Darling, I don't feel hungry.

3. The Great Poet Reconsiders the Generation of '68

after John Tranter

He looks back over the gravestones
and his eyes grow misty again:
We Did It Our Way, boys, he thinks,
oh, and you two girls.
We re-discovered things
that had not been re-discovered for . . .
well, months. How New it seemed, then,
like Sex perhaps, something else
we had to teach Them about—
however did the race survive this far?
His toke grows cold in the ashtray

as he stares down at his Collected Poems.
Collected Poems? *Moi*? A change of air
is what he needs, a week on the East Side
among the hum-coloured Puerto Ricans,
a cubby in the Museum of Fairly Modern Art.
Anything but this: poems on the Syllabus,
a seat on the Establishment,
an individual talent become Tradition,
no longer read,
but studied.

Two Sporting Elegies

1. *Rod Laver*

I remember those crystal set finals
in the small hours of childhood,
guiding unseen volleys home,
so proud of our small tribe,
our achievements with cat-gut and rubber balls.

And then the first year I forgot to listen,
you lost in the opening round;
the same year Patrick White
won through the semis in Stockholm.

Ah Rocket, poet of summer and lawn,
Ginger Meggs in white sandshoes,
I am finally growing up. Or merely old.
The strain of direct telecasts is beyond me,
I try to read Voss instead.

2. *Nadia Comaneci*

I sit at the piano with Mozart
in a convent in the past,
hearing football in the yard.

Sister rulers my knuckles
through a thousand scales,
friends kick goals outside.

It is always,
and never,
worth it.

You are starting the rest of your life.
After twenty-one years
of protein and somersaults,

after a second on the dais.
You are a violin of hard gristle,
a Heroine Of Labour, First Class, retired.

It is always,
and never,
worth it.

Trick Knee

More ice, please.
And less Kindness.
I have reached the age

of How's the Knee,
of Starting from the Bench.
The Best-and-Fairest statuettes

are gone, this season's end
brings a joke medallion only,
bearing an inscription. Very Funny:

Age And Treachery
Will Always Overcome
Youth And Skill

I sit in a Clubroom
with a knee on the rocks,
wanting to be nothing

except a boy forever.
Things learnt long ago
but held in zones of joke

are sinking in.
A week I spent
with both eyes bandaged.

A month at life's edge,
intensively cared,
my chest full of blood.

And always the Ankles
and Hamstrings,
and Thighs and Knees:

that crippled centipede
I trail endlessly behind me
through the Saturdays.

At the Filling
of the Hot Water Bottle,
and with the Morning Stiffness,

I remember these.
But sometimes—
grudgingly—also this:

a single Cup Final,
before a Crowd,
all relatives.

Plus—among the Safe,
the Solidly Reliable,
the Workmanlike—

a handful of sweetly
fluked dance-steps
that repeat in the mind

like stuck, unwanted tunes,
uselessly, obstinately,
lovely.

Mass for the Middle-Aged

1. *Lacrimosa*

Suddenly breakfast is over
and all the years before,

and my dog is dead,
and my children grown old.

It all seems so overnight,
like catching a death of something

or preferring Mozart:
the turning world slips

another ratchet-tooth,
and I awake, alarmed.

For the first time
regrets outnumber dreams.

To have been more useful.
To have fed the hungry

or persuaded the damned.
There was also that night

in the backseat at the Drive-in:
if only I had known.

2. Confutatis

Slowly the future grows cold,
the best water spills
over the edge, displaced,
the fear of death
becomes the longing for death,
the only sure resolution.

3. Libera Me

Deliver me, Lord, from the threat
of heaven, from becoming the angel
who is not me, who smiles
faintly, fondly

before shrugging me off
like some stiff, quaint pupal case:
the battered leather jacket of the flesh,
evidence of misspent youth.

Grant me, Lord, this last request:
to wear bikie colours in heaven,
a grub among the butterflies.
And this: to take all memories with me,

all memories that *are* me,
intact, seized first
like snapshot albums
from a burning house.

Answer, Lord, these prayers,
for I would rather
be nothing
than improved.

4. *In Paradisum*

With any luck heaven will be much
like here, now, on a good day: pleasant,
but not too, its joys unsaturated, its lusts
remaining, fractionally, lusts.
I see a kind of Swiss Patent Office
with time to think, and skylights.
Somewhere music teases, distant
as Latin, and the volumes on the shelves
are always one page too slim.
As promised, there will be no pain:
each bare nerve-end rewired instead
for tickle. At meal-times I will rise
from my small exquisite portions,
still hungry, just, and mildly restless,
forever.

Piano

Each night I return to this discipline:
a straight-back on a hard bench
in an unheated room, sometimes uncooled,
embarked on Czerny without end
or pun, an unsmiling bondage.

The piano is the heaviest thing
I own: heavier than a set of weights
or a complicated exercise machine, heavier
than a small car and travelling further.

Allowed inside it will not be ignored.
It expands to fill the biggest room.
A planet, it draws me
past armchairs, past cooling meals,
past better versions by other people
reproduced.

Yet it contains no music.
Nor are there images to be had inside:
no moonlight or sunken churches,
no picturesque exhibitions.
If I push back the lid I find
only notes: black and white,
loud and soft, sharp and flat.

The wrong alone are of interest:
as long as there is error
there is hope, there is a day's hard work,
there is perfection to be again disproved.

As for hands: a kind of mob
which must be broken.
This delinquent right index, that lazy left little.
Even you, thumbs—yes, you, in the middle—
have whittled toothpicks on demand,
have moved holes from here to here

as I sit upright, nightly:
stern-faced, rod-backed,
posed as if before a mirror
or on a starting-block, facing the music,
aiming to break the minute waltz.

Piano Stool

Silent night
in the composers' locked cell:

Frederic coughs, Old Bach snores,
Wolf lies down with Franz.

Even you, Claude
(yes, you—nearest the hatch,

first released,
last imprisoned each day),

sleep, finally, hidden
from all the moonlight

and watery noises.
Tomorrow

you will each be taken
separately

for exercise
and further questioning:

painful, perhaps,
but only to the ear;

for make no mistake,
one day you will sing

loudly, perfectly,
spilling everything,

and everything
will suddenly be clear.

Music

Legato of after-rain
on an iron roof, drop
following slow drop
exactly at the brink of disconnection.

Something is being stitched
together, but what?
Deceptive this seamless music,
and all the variations
of heartbeat, drumbeat
which repeat it.

I once thought music a gift
from places high and distant:
it seemed so pure,
so stupid. Later I blamed it
for everything: all those lies
set to waltz-time, all those
plausible feelings in a minor key,
invitations to a lynching.

And listening in private?
Ears blinkered with headphones,
or furtive Walkmans in the park?
Careful: the walls have ears.
Not even this—especially
not even this—is safe.
Nor this: the lengthening pause
between raindrops,
and in that pause
the continuo of human breathing,
an inflection of silence:

noise and hush,
noise and hush.

April 25th

Strumming through a folder
of convict ballads, found one
from the trenches of 1917.

The iron flutes of that war
are long beaten into ploughshares,
the voices ploughed into earth.

But the music survives—and I don't mean
in the forced march of brass bands
or hymns to pleasant English queens.

I mean in songs that are broken
like bread or rations.
Worn true by a thousand throats.

Passed down like the silence
that grew in me
those wet April mornings

in country schoolyards
ripped by wind and giggles
and the tuneless memories of a bugle.

A Shoeshine for Louis Armstrong

How perfectly
the gramophone remembers

your trumpet's sweet blasphemy,
the blackness of your voice;

a voice as black
and blue as I am green:

words can never have this ease
this happiness of lips on brass,

of fingers slipping into chords
like cool ivory gloves.

The air is slippery with jazz,
with perfectly remembered blues,

and all that words can do
is shine, shine your shoes.

Gustav Mahler:
Songs on the Death of Children

It's snowing in Adelaide
on the gramophone,
white hiss and static at 78rpm:
snowing in Vienna, in Adelaide.

It's snowing on a father's grief,
on a tear-smudged manuscript,
on a garret on Freudstrasse:
it's snowing on the soundtrack of your life.

It's snowing in Vienna, in Adelaide
until I lift the needle off,
and then it's fine and clear,

and your music walks away,
on snowshoes of slow violins,
into the silence of the air.

Richard Strauss: A Hero's Life

Somewhere in the silent circuits
—your deepest, darkest lobes—
decisions choose themselves.

The modern brain is binary,
its computations state-of-the-art:
easy black and white alternatives
separate you from responsibility.

For the mind is an electrical event
merely obeying orders,
right and wrong differ only in voltage

as music a weightless ocean
spills like piss from your skull,
that slop-filled chamberpot,
that frail, exquisite chalice.

Pablo Neruda

At autopsy the paperback
opens like a flap of scalp.
Pathologists bluntly dissect
the pages of brain, smirking
The Heights of Pablo Neruda
into their uniforms and medals.

Their bloodstained fingers
point out errors in structure
and metabolism not fit to survive
in a free enterprise biology,

and roll between thumb and finger
the vestigial soul, laughably small,
a useless appendage made perhaps
of love, extinct as bronze,
or poetry, a dead language.

But the poet survives
on a back cover photograph,
a gentle suburban communist
posed in his leatherbound library,
munching a United Fruit
under the lampshade.

Coast

At edge of sleep the colours of the world
run together, unreliably, like metaphors,
all categories re-open for business,
the due word processes of reason collapse.

Each night I doze alertly, watching
for the accidental, absent-minded repeal
of natural law, selecting visions
from the dreamy, streaky shapes.

I like this jaggy sawtooth state
at brink of dream: the jerk awake and drift
back and jerk awake, channel-hopping
very strange Late Late Shows.

There is no risk. One step back and I am safe
again, among things hardened
and separated by naming and science.
One step forward . . . sleep.

Meanwhile, this narrow littoral,
these volumes that merge and separate
and merge again without displacement,
this giddy double and triple-mindedness,

the various melodies, known and unknown,
hinting at a final chord, when the horizontal
at last becomes vertical, and movement ceases;
the nearest thing to simultaneity, perhaps, This Side.

Suicide on Christmas Eve

After the doctor, the steam-cleaners,
more usefully. I drive home to bed
through intersections sequinned with glass:
it's Christmas Eve, season of donor organs.

What is the meaning of life? I shake you
gently awake. What answer would satisfy?
you mumble, yawning, from Your Side.
To understand is to be bored, you say,
practising, perhaps, for Speech Night.
Knowledge is a kind of exhaustion, you say.

A child enters our room: is it morning yet?
Not Yet. In another room the lights of the Tree
wink colourfully, and when the telephone rings
again, it is almost, but not quite, in time.

Fragments of Grandpa

1.

Piano player at the old Ozone, honky
tonking between Chaplin and Keaton
till replaced by a Wurlitzer.

First of bikies;
only after a dozen write-offs
condemned to Morris Minors,
and even then racing locomotives
across the tracks.

Episodic maniac. At first
a torrent of wit and words,
later only weeping and violence,
security wards and shock therapy.

And always this narrowing
of exits. We never met, these myths
I have constructed from hints,
fragments of a kinship.

2.

The man I knew
live in a drugged autumn,
a spare-room banishment
spent

playing model trains,
coughing and farting
among motorbike magazines,

and walking grandchildren
to the crossing each night,
the Melbourne Express
dieselling through a haze
of largactil and memories.

O jazzplayer of legend,
psychotic and bikie,
however did you die
of old age?

Ecclesiastes

Give me no more lessons of history.
No more fatherlands or economics.
Enough words.

My head is choked with their gristle.
With too many lies. With words
that kill children who have no words.

A scream was the first word,
and will be the last, the grammar of pain
dissolving under tongues of earth.

If at all, let language be better than this:
as pure as the verbs of algebra,
or the distance of tongues.

Or louder than words—
burning books, attacking trees,
consuming the air that cruelly allows speech.

Like defeated kings
putting oceans to the sword—
one more lesson of history.

My Last Rabbit

My first rabbit was the hardest.
Unscrewing the neck,
flipping gut-things between my legs.
Later I developed forehand,
and the traps set themselves.

And then my first two-legged corpse,
my first day in dissection.
There was cold pork for dinner, inevitably—
but coming up hot later.
I never ate meat again—till the next week.

I should mention also a slaughterhouse
downwind from memory.
A place I might have visited,
or might have not. It was all long ago.

Because always this forgetting.
This bringing kill home in butcher's paper,
picked like fruit off a shelf,
smothered with herbs and euphemisms
till it could be anything.

At times I seem almost to remember
the sealed trucks arriving,
the sheep hurrying to be meat.
At times I count them at night,
trying to stay awake.

A Statistician to His Love

Men kill women in bedrooms, usually
by hand, or gun. Women kill men,
less often, in kitchens, with knives.
Don't be alarmed, there is understanding
to be sucked from all such hard
and bony facts, or at least a sense
of symmetry. Drowned men—an
instance—float face down, women up.
But women, ignited, burn more fiercely.
The death camp pyres were therefore,
sensibly, women and children first,
an oily kind of kindling. The men
were stacked in rows on top. Yes,
there is always logic in this world.
And neatness. And the comfort
of fact. Did I mention that suicides
outnumber homicides? Recent figures
are reliable. So stay awhile yet
with me: the person to avoid, alone,
is mostly you yourself.

Cimetiere Pere Lachaise

1.

Even in Paris graveyards there are queues: tourists
clutching phrase-books and muttering the Basic Expression:
If Only There Weren't So Many Tourists.
Officials sell roses and a map of fashionable tombs:
the whereabouts of celebrities, more famous for being dead.
I wander among rows of upright granite phone-booths,
checking Names and Dates and Numbers. At Oscar's
the crowd is thickest: a line of men waiting to phone home.
At Gertrude's? Only women, who watch me suspiciously.
Music and the sound of heated English draws me to another
    plot
thick with anglophones: teenage backpackers swigging wine
and listening to a cassette of The Doors. No phone-booth
    here,
the grave is flat; a broken rock, a hewn name: *Jim Morrison.*
He was my age, I tell them. None of you were born.
Jim Lives a child says, and passes me a bottle.
I sit and sip and listen to the noise of Resurrection:
The Body Didn't Look Like Jim. The Death Certificate
Was Forged. Someone Saw Him, Risen, In Galilee . . .
The horizontal door, a granite slab, stays shut, the cassette
    ends.
Lennon was killed by the CIA, someone mutters;
the worshippers disperse, wanting to believe, and finding
    it easy.

2.

I remember when it was easy. I remember
my first shave with Ockham: everything
is a conspiracy. For a time I sit alone
among the Gauloise stubs and scattered empties
and disconnected stone phone-boxes.
The past is a text, I read this morning
in a book review in last night's *Paris Soir*.
If so its words are difficult to read, a text
cleansed of conjunctions. Unconnected things
come back, scattered across distant pages:
school, too many years ago, and drunken weekend nights,
and Jim—and Jimi, and Janis—and someone else now gone,
a girl I knew who set odd precious nights on fire.
Perhaps a cemetery far from home is no fit place
to flip back through the past, but everywhere
of late seems far from home, including home.
So many things have gone unimportant,
so many lusts and angers have come to seem
fake orgasms, like wearing a black armband
the day that Hendrix died, feeling a public sadness
I'd never privately earned. These days I prefer Chopin,
his grave is over there. As for seasonal beliefs,
I have no faith in resurrection, or in anything else right now
except the need for tidiness. I rise and bin my bottle,
and walk away clutching my map of the dead
and my single long-stem rose, bypassing Gertrude and Oscar,
searching somewhere between Chopin's grave
and Proust's, for the Tomb of the Homesick Tourist,
open-doored, perhaps, as if ready to receive.

After the Ball

Late-risen, we sit near breakfast
reading large, simple sentences;
outside the remains of Sunday shine
as uselessly as a halfholiday.
Compensation Shock, you read aloud.
How can money bring back our son—
we expected twice as much.
Baffling, yes—but anything smaller
than headlines feels too complex
or hurts the eyes. *Victim Cheated*
At Scrabble, Murderer Claims.
You avert your gaze, suddenly giddy,
trying to fix on more distant points.
Music helps: a proper soundtrack
can ennoble the cheapest movie,
change even weekdays into sabbaths.
For a time we listen, remembering
previous listenings, knowing
that beyond clarinet-range the world
continues, as picturesque as poverty.
Once we visited it, many Sundays ago,
holding hands, walking through Scenery,
giving thanks that between the act
and the consequence comes the excuse,
always, and that learning still offers
the best defence against knowledge.
Church bells ring in the far blue, gently
itching, but these Sunday mornings
we believe in nothing, not even in Love:
our flesh does that for us, and more.
The only certainty, we joke, are jokes:
one day we *will* be seen dead in church.
And if jokes also are a form of headline,
what matter? Where is the sin
in wanting to read no further,

in refusing to wonder what thinking is like
before we begin to talk about it,
or what a feeling—any feeling—might mean
the last instant before it simples into words?

The Grasshopper Heart

ANDREW LANSDOWN

...I go back, not to the poem
in progress, but to a new poem, this poem,
as a man who has been blessed returns
to his business but cannot resume
business-as-usual, being unsettled by calm.

Many of Andrew Lansdown's poems have the power to bless, to unsettle now with mysterious calm, now with the deep resonance of poetry. Of all Australian imagists, he is the one with the broadest and warmest human sympathy, and no one writes of family love with more tenderness than he. Nor does anyone write with more perceptive courage about the dark things that move behind idyll, or the bland merciless enemies of human happiness.

'Lansdown is a past master at performing one of the chief tasks of a serious poet: to lift the veil of familiarity from the world, to have us see things anew, to re-encounter what we thought we had understood, and to take another look at what we might have consigned to the margins of our consciousness.'

Rod Moran, FREMANTLE ARTS REVIEW

Paperweight

John Foulcher

This is the darkest of John Foulcher's three collections of poems. In the arresting title poem he writes, 'the other, beautiful paperweights/have become unnecessary. This one/has them all... The whole room/ is embossed on it, and the colours are shrouded in black,/the way a candle burns within the night/ as if forever...' And who indeed can put it better than the poet himself?

In exploring this new ground, Foulcher has developed and deepened the imagistic richness his work has always shown, and his voice becomes steadily more distinctive, a strong presence in Australian poetry.

Selected Poems

GWEN HARWOOD

Gwen Harwood was born in Brisbane in 1920. Keenly interested in music, she was to teach music and serve for a time as organist at All Saints' Church, Brisbane. Married with four children, she is now a grandmother and pursues many interests including the study of modern philosophy and working with composers.

This revised edition of *Selected Poems* incorporates her acclaimed collection, *Bone Scan*, which won the 1989 Victorian Premier's Literary Award for poetry. Other awards received by Gwen Harwood include the Grace Levin Prize 1975, the Robert Frost Award 1977 and the Patrick White Award 1978. In 1988 she received an Honorary Doctorate of Letters from the University of Tasmania.

The Earthquake Lands

Hal Colebatch

'A genuine poet... here is the true rebel of the 1980s.'
C.J. Koch, SYDNEY MORNING HERALD

The Earthquake Lands, Hal Colebatch's fourth volume, is a poetry of satire and celebration, anger and hope. While his world can be peopled with monsters, it is also filled with beauty and delight and a sense of the wonder of things. This is the poetry of post-modern man, facing the future with both optimism and fear, yet acutely aware of the heritage of the past and the unity of human experience. It celebrates human heroism and the natural world, its celebration sometimes offset by savage indignation.

Hal Colebatch is a poet of unconventional hope, courageously working to break poetry out of its twentieth-century ghetto, so as to reach again the wide audience it has had in other ages.

From the Midnight Courtyard

ELIZABETH RIDDELL

Elizabeth Riddell has not been a prolific poet, but the poems of her smallish oeuvre have often stayed with readers for decades. Several are already essential parts of the Australian literary heritage. Raised in New Zealand, long resident in Australia, she is always a distinctive writer, her poems continually achieving fresh approaches as they move back and forth across the Tasman. Carefully chosen and arranged by the poet herself, in an order which, rather than merely chronological, is in fact intrinsic to her writing and its inner life, this book distils the work of a lifetime, and restores to readers a wealth of fine-grained achievement.

Selected Poems

ERIC ROLLS

Eric Rolls was born in Grenfell in 1923. He has been involved with the land for most of his life and believes that 'the soil is the perfect background for a writer'. Until 1986 he farmed full-time at Cumberdeen, Baradine, where he still lives and where he has written most of his award-winning histories, including *They All Ran Wild* and *A Million Wild Acres*, and celebrations of Australian life.

Selected Poems, drawn from two previously published volumes and occasional publishing over more than fifty years, demonstrates his gift for nature lyrics as well as satire and irony.